Looking at
Animals
in
the
OCEAN

Moira Butterfield

Belitha Press

Introduction

There are many oceans around the world. They stretch for thousands of miles. Some parts of the ocean are very deep and dark, while other parts are so shallow you can see the bottom.

Hundreds of different animals live in the oceans, from brightly-coloured coral to dangerous sharks. Some live near the bottom of the ocean, some live near the top. Some are the size of your hand, others are the size of an aeroplane.

All these animals need to be able to swim and find food. Every animal has its own way of living in the ocean.

2/2/17

Looking at
Animals
in
the
OCEAN

First published in Great Britain in 1999 by
Belitha Press Limited,
London House, Great Eastern Wharf,
Parkgate Road, London SW11 4NQ

This paperback edition first published in 2000

Copyright © Belitha Press Limited 1999
Text copyright © Moira Butterfield 1999

Series Editor Honor Head
Series Designer Hayley Cove
Picture Researcher Juliet Duff
Map Artwork Robin Carter / Wildlife Art Agency
Animal Symbols Arlene Adams

ISBN 1 84138 159 4 (paperback)
ISBN 1 84138 146 2 (big book)
ISBN 1 84138 022 9 (hardback)

Printed in China

10 9 8 7 6 5 4 3 2 1

British Library Cataloguing in Publication Data
for this book is available from the British Library

Photographic credits
Frank Lane Picture Picture Agency: 12 J Nahmens/Earthviews;
14 K Aitken/Panda; 15 Ian Cartwright; 27 D Fleetman/Silvestris.
NHPA: 7 Daniel Heuclin; 26 Trevor McDonald. Oxford Scientific Films:
6 Max Gibbs; 8, 9 Richard Herrmann; 11 Peter Parks; 13 David Fleetham;
19, 22 Howard Hall; 20 Paul Kay; 21 Colin Milkins; 29 Kathie Atkinson.
Planet Earth Pictures: 10, 28 Peter Scoones; 16 Marty Snyderman;
17 Pete Atkinson; 18, 23 Gary Bell; 24, 25 Doug Perrine.
Cover
Oxford Scientific Films: top left Paul Kay; top right Max Gibbs.
Planet Earth Pictures: bottom Gary Bell.

Contents

Seahorse

A seahorse has a head that makes it look like a real horse. It has a long curly tail that it can wrap around seaweed. It has tiny see-through fins.

Its fins look as though they are made of tissue paper. The seahorse swims along by fanning them to and fro very quickly.

Tuna

Tuna fish have shiny silvery scales all over their bodies. Their long, thin shape helps them to swim very fast through the water. They live in big groups called shoals. Tuna fish are good to eat so fishing boats hunt for the shoals and try to catch the tuna in nets.

Jellyfish

Jellyfish have see-through bodies that look as though they are made of jelly. They float around dangling their long thin arms called tentacles.

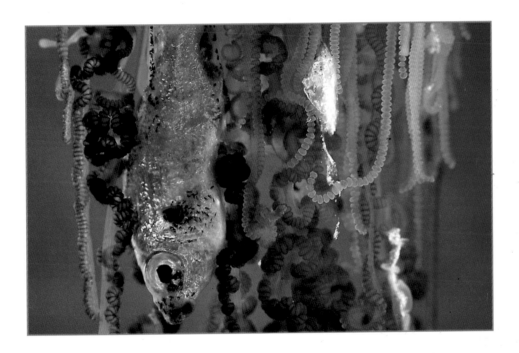

The tentacles have stings on them that kill small animals. The jellyfish pushes the animal into its mouth to eat it.

Whale

Whales sometimes breach, which means they leap up out of the water. They are very long and heavy, so they make a big splash. When they are ready to dive they flip their giant tails up into the air. Then they swim down to the bottom of the sea to find food.

Coral

Corals look like underwater rocks or plants, but they are really made of lots of tiny animals. They all live together in one place called a coral reef.

Some corals look like trees. Some are round-shaped like balls and some spread out like pretty, feathery fans.

Manta ray

A manta ray has a wide, flat body like
a giant pancake. It swims by flapping
up and down through the water, and
it collects food at the same time. As
the ray moves along it keeps its mouth
open to catch tiny animals called
plankton which float in the sea water.

Shark

Sharks have sharp teeth like rows of little pointed knives. There are lots of different kinds of sharks. The hammerhead shark is one of the fiercest in the ocean.

It has a big, wide head shaped like the end of a hammer. It uses it for bashing into other animals it wants to kill and eat.

Starfish

The starfish has lots of tiny tubes along each one of its arms. The tubes are its feet. It uses them to move along or to grip rocks. The starfish grabs animals in its arms and puts them in its mouth, which is underneath its body. If it loses an arm it can grow a new one.

Octopus

An octopus has eight tentacles with suckers all along them. It uses its tentacles to swim along. It creeps up on other animals and then jumps on them.

It wraps its tentacles around them and eats them. Some octopuses are brightly coloured to show that they are poisonous.

Dolphin

Dolphins swim around in families. They are very clever and they talk to each other with clicking and squeaking noises. They play together and help each other. If a dolphin is ill other dolphins will help it to float along until it is better.

Butterfly fish

Butterfly fish live around coral reefs.
There are lots of different kinds. Some
have a flat, round body like a plate. They
are all brightly coloured like butterflies.

If another fish like them swims by, they
see that it is the same colour as them
and they know it is a friend, not an enemy.

Sea cucumber

A sea cucumber doesn't hunt other animals. It eats leftovers. It crawls along the sea bed looking for tiny bits of food to collect on its sticky tentacles. Then it puts its tentacles into its mouth and sucks them. Sea cucumbers grow in lots of different shapes and colours.

Where they live

This map of the world shows you where the animals live.

 seahorse

 tuna

 jellyfish

 whale

 coral

 manta ray

 shark

 hammerhead shark

 starfish

 octopus

 dolphin

 butterfly fish

 sea cucumber

NORTH AMERICA

PACIFIC OCEAN

SOUTH AMERICA

ARCTIC OCEAN

ASIA

EUROPE

PACIFIC OCEAN

AFRICA

INDIAN OCEAN

AUSTRALIA

ATLANTIC OCEAN

SOUTHERN OCEAN

Index of words to learn

coral reef a long line of coral under

the sea 15, 27

fins pointed parts on a fish's body.

They help the fish to swim along 7

plankton tiny creatures, too small for us

to see, that float in water 17

scales tiny overlapping pieces of skin that

cover a fish's body 9

shoal a big group of fish swimming together . 9

suckers round shapes on an animal's

body used to grip things 23

tentacles long, thin arms with no hands

or feet on the end 11, 23, 29